THE

LOST

ARCANA

PAUL

MCCARTHY

To contact the Author

You can contact the author by email at
guidedbythelight@hotmail.com
Website: https://newarcanatarot.com/

Contents

Introduction

There are many mysteries surrounding the origins of Tarot and how playing cards evolved into the popular tool for divination and spiritual guidance. Did they originate in ancient Egypt as believed by the members of the Golden Dawn and Edward Arthur Waite, the creator of the leading Rider-Waite-Coleman Tarot cards? Do the cards imbue the reader with psychic powers? Arcana means mystery or secrets. Whilst these are fascinating subjects, for me, the greatest secret is that the energies and spiritual realities that Tarot cards highlight, exist independently in the world, and are not just associated with Tarot cards and their readings. Tarot cards point to a reality that existed long before they were created. So where do else we find these Tarot energies?

Ley Lines possess highly spiritual and universal energies which, are, in fact, the same as the Major Arcana energies. These are, in part, described in Tarot. Each ley line consists of two lines of energy in the form of a male line energy and a female energy. Each one is overprinted with a different Major Arcana energy. These two Major Arcana energies create spiritual themes that we can experience in their presence. They draw to them those people who need their energetic support with the spiritual themes they represent.

Often, this happens in a subconscious manner, but after reflection, we can often see that there is no coincidence as to why a person visits, lives or works in an area that is a host to a specific ley line. They needed to be in that specific energy and not another.

Another example of the existence of Major Arcana Tarot energies is found when we explore our soul's purpose. As individual souls, we are all overprinted with one of the Major Arcana card energies, as described in Tarot cards. All souls know these energies found on the soul plane, as we merge with one of the energies of the Major Arcana cards. It also forms our path of learning, our life missions, and influences how we will express our spirituality on Earth. I have always been aware of different energies of souls on the soul plane, and how they belong to different groups. These groups are identified by the different arcana energies. This is one of the reasons why we are mysteriously attracted to certain people, given that we resonate with their shared imprinted arcana energies. Each group represents one of the twenty-two Major Arcana energies. I am aware of more than the traditional twenty-two Major Arcana energies, and I call these "The Lost Arcana", as they are currently not known to humanity, but were probably known to the ancients in times of enlightenment.

Major Arcana energies are linked to many important aspects of our lives. We are spiritually and energetically linked to a variety of them, and we interact with them in different areas of life. For example, a business will have an over-lighting Major Arcana energy, which is directly linked to its founder(s) and its purpose. Knowing which arcana energy this is, can help us to understand its real qualities, gifts, and potential. Our partners and children also have Major Arcana energies linked to their lives which indirectly affect our lives too.

The "Lost Arcana" energies are Major Arcana energies, but they are the 15 additional ones that are currently unknown to humanity, but which I am revealing in this book. There is a big difference however between these and the previously known Major Arcana energies portrayed in Tarot decks (cards 0 – 21). These Tarot cards refer to energies that influence us spiritually including themes such as karma, fate, and polarity. The pattern of the new Lost Arcana energies is to help facilitate opportunities to break free of the normal restrictions that a physical being experiences when they incarnate into the physical universe. These include "transcending karma", "fate", and "polarity". These are profound opportunities that many might have never thought were possible. The Lost Arcana energies show us how to experience and explore pure spiritual realities at the highest levels. These new themes will be of interest to those who explore higher consciousness, ascension and instinctively feel there is something awaiting them that will give them the tools to liberate themselves

3

from these restrictions. For those of you who feel magnetically drawn to Tarot cards, and who may not even use them for readings, please trust your feelings as they are guiding you to a deeper reality linked to Tarot cards. I hope that the Lost Arcana will open a door to you and show you something quite special that you might have been waiting for.

My use of Tarot cards is clearly different from traditional Tarot card readers, who use the cards for divination whereas I use them to understand human spiritual consciousness. The Tarot cards point to energies of the soul which are also found in Ley Lines, and I am using them to explore these realities rather than to make predictions about the future. I am not saying that Tarot cards cannot be used for divination as in the hands of a skilled psychic they are useful, it is just that this is not their primary benefit. The truth of what the Tarot energies represent can be revealed by tuning into the individual cards and feeling their original spiritual energies that tell the stories of the soul's journey on Earth. In this way, the Tarot cards revealed to me spiritual truths and realities much greater than the modern-day interpretations of the cards. Studying these energies led me to discoveries about the Lost Arcana energies. Indeed, Arthur Edward Waite, the creator of the leading *Rider Waite Smith* Tarot deck mirrored my thoughts on this subject. In his autobiography *Shadows of Life and*

Thought, and referring to his illustrator Pamela Coleman Smith, he writes,

> "It seemed to some of us in the circle that there was a draughtswoman amongst us who, under proper guidance, could produce a Tarot with an appeal in the world of art and a suggestion of significance behind the symbols which would put on them another construction than had ever been dreamed of by those who, through many generations, had produced and used them for mere divination purposes. My province was to see that the designs – especially those of the important Trump majors - kept that in the hiddenness which belongs to certain greater mysteries, in the paths of which I was traveling."

I can think of no greater confirmation of my thoughts that Tarot is much more than a divination system than having the creator of the modern-day Tarot say so himself. It is unlikely that Arthur Waite realised that the energies of the Tarot are present in the Ley Lines, since the subject of Ley Lines was not even introduced until 1925, and after the publication of his Tarot cards. Without his work with Pamela Coleman Smith, it would make my realisation of this connection between the Tarot, Ley Lines, and the Soul much harder to come by. For this, I am very grateful to Arthur and Pamela.

My goal with working with the Lost Arcana energies is to tune into their energies and describe these as accurately as possible. As with all spiritual energies, their energies reveal exactly what their functions and qualities are. Major Arcana energies can be read like a spiritual "bar code " if we approach them in the right way. If we want to understand such things this approach will give us the clearest and deepest insights. As with the traditional Major Arcana energies, they have a purpose and influence us in specific ways. The information I provide in this book focuses on the spiritual effect of these energies on human beings, as this specific information is not currently available.

How am I sensing the Major Arcana energies? I have a sensitivity to the presence of all spiritual energies, developed in a career working with the leading New Age subjects of star seeds, energy work, channelling, healing, and crystals. Over the past twenty-three years, I have developed the skills to identify spiritual energies and define their purpose and effects on humans. To truly feel spiritual energies is to merge with them and have a spiritual experience from which we can gain insights and build up observations about them. These experiences allow me to recognise the different Major Arcana energies and understand what these energies represent, and how they affect us. Every person can develop their sensitivity to the Major Arcana energies and to spiritual energies in general.

The ability to sense the qualities of these energies is almost as important as being able to sense their presence.

The levels of human awareness of unseen spiritual realities are, in part, linked to the general energetic and spiritual conditions on Earth. There are times when energies and consciousness are high, and so humans feel the presence of these energies more easily. I call this pattern the cycles of consciousness. Conversely, there are times when energies and consciousness are relatively low on Earth and humans tend to lose their ability to sense and connect to spiritual and energic realities. Humanity is currently leaving the low point of a downwards cycle and since 2012 energies are rising once again. In theory, people should now start to become more sensitive to spiritual energies. As a spiritual teacher, I can confirm this to be true from my own observations. Many of my clients are experiencing rapid advances in spiritual consciousness, which will lead to new levels of sensitivity to spiritual realities. I cannot claim responsibility for all this progress, and I recognise that we are all receiving an incredible surge of higher spiritual energies and growth opportunities. It means we are starting to be able to sense and recognise higher spiritual realities which have not been possible for many humans since the last cycle, which ended in the times of Atlantis over 10,000 years ago. In a short time, many more people will be able to sense the energies of Ley Lines and Soul energies as I do today. This will result in some people experiencing spiritual realities soon that have not been possible for thousands of years. These will be linked to the higher Lost Arcana energies that are starting to come in. These should be described in Tarot as cards numbers 22-36. The purpose of my book is to introduce and define these, so that there is a reference for those who seek to understand these higher Major Arcana energies and how they affect their human spiritual consciousness.

Discovering The Lost Major Arcana Energies

The twenty-two Major Arcana Tarot card set is incomplete and there are at least 15 more Major Arcana energies that could be represented by new Tarot cards. This chapter explains how I came to the realisation that there are Tarot cards that are missing, why placing these energies into groups of twelve works, and describes the new higher Major Arcana energies.

The first clue to the missing Tarot cards comes from another divination system called the Runes. These ancient symbols come from the ancient Germanic tribes and the Vikings. Like Tarot, they are commonly used for divination purposes, but they also have a deeper spiritual meaning. For example, it is believed that different Norse Gods ruled different groups of runes each of which represented a magic initiatory practice. When I tune into their energies, I feel the same energies as Tarot cards. As such the Tarot card called the Magician and numbered 1 carries the same energies as the Elder Futhark rune symbol called Fehu which is also numbered 1. The second Tarot card called the High Priestess has the same energies as the second rune symbol called Uruz and so on.

The runes of the Elder Futhark contain twenty-four individual runes which, in turn, correspond to the Major Arcana Tarot cards in terms of their energies. The Tarot cards, however, stop at card number twenty-one which is called the World. This is the first clue as to there being a shortfall in the number of Major Arcana Tarot cards. If these different systems mirror each other then why does one of them have more components than the other? Indeed, with the later extended thirty-three Anglo-Saxon runic set, we are shown there are even more Major Arcana energies that are not currently represented in the Tarot.

So, if the runes contain more energies, then should we all use the runes instead of Tarot? I would suggest that the Tarot cards are more useful, as the modern-day cards are based on the Rider Waite Smith cards which are about one hundred years old compared to the runes of the Elder Futhark, which are about eighteen hundred years old. The interpretations of the Tarot cards are more modern and helpful than the much older interpretations of the runes. The language and philosophy used with runes represent a world that is unrecognisable to us in modern times. Indeed, when reading the cultural interpretations of the runes, I struggle to reconcile these with the original spiritual energies of the runes. A system to help us understand the energies must give us descriptions of the energies which are recognisable and useful to us in the modern world, and in this area I believe Tarot is better suited for this than the runes. In addition, although the Anglo-Saxon runes go up to number thirty-three, I am aware of at least thirty-six Major Arcana energies and so the runes also represent an incomplete system in terms of understanding higher Arcana energies, and, ultimately, human spiritual consciousness.

Aside from the clues mentioned above, I noticed other anomalies with the structure of the Tarot in terms of the number of cards representing different parts of the decks. The Minor Arcana cards are currently divided into four groups of eleven cards, plus four court cards. Traditionally the Major Arcana Tarot cards are placed into a group of twenty-two. Instinctively, these groups did not feel right to me, as I felt the numbers of the Minor Arcana should be reflected in the numbers of the Major Arcana cards, which they do not. I started exploring how Tarot would work energetically if I placed the cards into groups that more accurately reflect their energies and meanings. I was led to place the cards into groups of twelve. We see groups of twelve in many spiritual structures, including twelve astrology signs and the twelve nodes of the Tree of Life. In the books by the hypnotherapist Michael Newton, he reports that during his sessions his clients state that souls belong to groups of twelve, which is important to my research, as the Major Arcana energies also link to the soul. As a musician, I am used to working with twelve intervals

11

in a scale, and I recognise that music also mirrors the journey of the soul. I see the groups of twelve everywhere in spiritual teachings, so this guided me to see if this applies to the Tarot energies. I started with the Major Arcana cards. Here the first group of twelve would be cards 1 - 12. The next group of twelve would be the Major Arcana group of cards 13 – 21, which is clearly missing three cards in modern Tarot decks.

As there is evidence that there are missing Major Arcana energies beyond what the Major Arcana Tarot cards currently represented, I tuned into this question and immediately received the energies and information of an additional fifteen Major Arcana energies. Therefore, I can share with you not only the missing three Major Arcana energies, but also that another grouping of 12 Lost Arcana energies exist.

My Groupings of Arcana Energies

Galactic Level – "Lost Arcana"	12 new Major Arcana cards "Lost Arcana" numbered 25-36
Spiritual Level	Major Arcana cards numbered 13-21+ 3 new ones (22,23 & 24)
Etheric Level	Major Arcana cards 1-12
Energies of the Elements	Minor Arcana cards 0-10 for each suit

The Energy of the Elements

The elements are the building blocks of spiritual energies and correspond to the Minor Arcana energies and the suits in the Tarot. These are the elements of water, air, fire, and earth. These spiritual energies are the closest to the physical realms and make us feel vibrant and alive. In their presence, we feel invigorated in ways that other spiritual energies including healing energies do not achieve. These Minor Arcana energies influence us in ways that are highlighted by Tarot cards.

Etheric Energies

Beyond the energies of the elements, we find Etheric energies. These represent the next higher energy, which is the bridge between the physical and the spiritual. In these energies, we feel a sense of dissolution, as if our sense of self(ego) is dissolving and we are merging with other energies. Energies at this level can be described as ethereal and otherworldly. In Tarot, these Etheric energies are represented by the first grouping of twelve Major Arcana cards numbered 1 -12, or the Magician card through to the Hanged Man card. It is the Etheric energy that often presents the major theme for the male and female Ley Lines and will be supported and complemented by the energies of the elements. I call it the "New Age" energy, as it pulls us in and invites us to go deeper, looking for something that the energy "promises". New-Age shops carry a similar energy, which creates this magical atmosphere.

Spiritual Energies

These energies are even more expansive than the previous grouping. Within Tarot, these higher spiritual energies are represented by the second grouping of Major Arcana cards numbered 13 -21, or The Death card through to The World cards. In addition, I have added 3 new "Lost Arcana" cards numbered 22-24 to complete this group of 12. These are a higher level of spiritual energies. In these high energies, we feel spirit and celestial realities.

Galactic Energies

These are the Lost Arcana cards, and they represent new energies and highly spiritual experiences for humanity. I call these "Galactic", as they introduce patterns of spiritual growth that are beyond planetary ascension. These energies are truly profound and represent the levels of spiritual consciousness that we associate with Masters such as Merlin and Mary Magdalene.

Why arranging the Tarot in groups of twelve works

In my explorations, I sensed the collective energies of each group of twelve cards, and I could see that placing them in groups of twelve works energetically. Here are some examples:

1. The energy of each group of twelve cards is higher than the preceding group. As we rise from one level to another, the spiritual experience of interacting with the energies of that group grows deeper and more expansive as you would expect. This pattern is also mirrored with the runes where the first three groups are called *aettir* or *aetts*. These groups represent aspects of human experience that progressively become more spiritual, as they advance from one group to the next.

2. For each Major Arcana card, using my arrangement, the corresponding card that is one octave higher in the next higher group of twelve, resonates energetically with the lower equivalent. Indeed, the combined energy of the two octave cards creates an ecstatic spiritual presence more powerful than the energies of the two cards combined. This is not true if we simply combine any two random Major Arcana Cards. This tells me that the "octave" cards are linked to each other, confirming that the structure of these energies belongs in groups of twelve. For example, the World Tarot card energy (number 21) is one octave higher than the Hermit Tarot card energy (number 9). To find the octave Tarot cards just add or subtract 12 from their assigned number.

You may ask why these additional Lost Arcana energies are not represented by modern-day Tarot cards. A raised consciousness is needed to even detect the energies and understand the concepts that these new Tarot energies bring. This level of human spiritual consciousness has not been present on Earth for thousands of years. Despite all the political and human drama that currently dominates our world, some human beings have rapidly raised their consciousness by an incredible amount recently. From a New-Age ascension point of view, they have completed their planetary ascension and are now moving into galactic ascension. This is what these new cards describe, and so were not relevant in the past or at least for the past ten thousand years. Before this time certainly, those who lived at the time, of Atlantis and other periods of raised consciousness would be more aware of these missing Major Arcana energies.

You may have noticed that I have not referred to the Fool Card numbered 0 from the traditional Tarot cards. When I tune into its pure energy, I sense the soul plane itself and not an Earthly connection. Therefore, this card represents the pure soul before its journey to Earth. As such, I do not include it in my groups of 12 or as a Major Arcana card, given the fact that its energies do not interact with us in the same way that the other Major Arcana energies do.

How to use The Lost Arcana Images and Information

After thoroughly exploring the energies of the individual Lost Arcana energies, I created a new Tarot-like card for each one with a focused description of its energies and how it interacts with our human spiritual consciousness. It was not necessary to create Tarot-like cards, but, like a lot of people, I am greatly attracted to Tarot and Oracle cards in general, as they help to bring alive the subjects they describe. My new Tarot-like images in this book are designed to hold the energies of each missing Tarot card, so that you can sense these energies as you look at each "card" and read the description. I have presented these as images in a book rather than as traditional Tarot cards, since they should not be used for divination, and by creating a typical Tarot-like card set, I would possibly be encouraging this. The "cards" in the book are designed to be used as a tool to explore spiritual energies and consciousness. I might create Tarot-like energy cards, which can be held, but this is to explore the energies and not to give readings with. I am not against people giving readings in general, as I do this type of work myself. It is just that to use the Lost Arcana energies in this way would mis represent their true nature.

The artwork contained in the cards help to symbolise the theme of each card, but they alone do not hold the energies. I attune the energies to each card using my intention.

Like the traditional Major Arcana energies highlighted in the Tarot, these higher Lost Arcana energies are essentially soul "packages". They are energies that promote specific spiritual experiences that lead us to grow in certain directions. They influence our spiritual motivations, gifts, and growth patterns. I see them as advanced soul packages that after we evolve sufficiently, can emerge into our lives to work alongside our original soul-imprinted Major Arcana energy. If you are somewhat spiritually evolved, it is your destiny to encounter these Lost Arcana energies, and they will come to you when the time is right. At the time of writing of this book, as I was tuning into the individual energies of the Lost Arcana cards, I recognised most of them as energies that had been coming into my life in the preceding months.

The Lost Arcana energies and the experiences associated with them, will come to the more evolved spiritual students regardless of which existing spiritual practices they are familiar with. As such, I am encouraging readers to develop their own relationship to the individual Lost Arcana energies as the simplest, most direct way to engage with these new opportunities rather than to try and fit this new information into existing systems and models apart from Tarot itself.

Although the Lost Arcana energies are numbered on the same basis as the traditional Major Arcana card of Tarot, it is important not to jump to conclusions about what this means. We do not necessarily encounter the Lost Arcana energies in sequential ways. Whilst I expect people to be initially drawn to the energies at the beginning of the range, it is entirely possible that they will move between the different energies in no specific order, depending on their own spiritual agenda. Whilst it is true that each higher grouping of Major Arcana cards and energies reflect more evolved spiritual content, within the groups themselves, higher number cards are not necessarily more spiritual in nature than lower numbered cards. Numerology plays its role with Major Arcana energies, and the number of each card, in part, reflects this connection, rather than to place it in a hierarchical structure.

The astrological alignments are with stars and constellations of stars whose natural energies promote similar spiritual experiences. Traditional Tarot cards link to specific planets and astrological signs for analogous reasons. As these Lost Arcana are more Galactic in nature, then we find the stars that resonate with the energies are outside our local solar system. These alignments are the ones that I know of, but it does not mean they are the only ones. There are most probably similar alignments to other stars and constellations of stars. It is important to note that the astrological alignments do not create the Major Arcana energies, as they are independent spiritual energies. They are more like physical expressions of them in the psychical universe. For me the pure Major Arcana energies give us a purer and more powerful experience of the spiritual themes they represent when compared to astrological alignments. We do not need to understand or use astrology to work with Major Arcana energies, but if you can see common realities in the different systems, it can be useful.

You can use the new card images in different ways:

1. They represent a library of higher energies and potential spiritual experiences which can be studied.
2. You can tune into the energies and sense how they interact with you, and how they activate spiritual growth.
3. You can use them as a reference so that when you experience new levels of spiritual energies and consciousness, you can better understand the themes involved.

The notes and descriptions for the cards refer to advanced spiritual themes. Some readers may not be familiar with the information and might need to carry out some private research to understand the content. There are different New

Age spiritual philosophies reflected in the information, and although it is not my intention to give encyclopaedic definitions for these, I have made some brief notes below which might be helpful. Certainly, I would recommend studying Tarot in general and, especially, from a spiritual perspective. After completing this book, I will be writing such a book, which I will be calling *Soul Imprinted Tarot*.

However, I do not recommend students of these subjects undertaking too much research. These higher spiritual realities are meant to be experienced in their totality, and not just mentally dissected. This book encourages this approach as the Tarot style images carry energies and are intended to be used as a meditation tool. The energies will activate those that are open to them and sensitise the reader to their presence. Whilst some knowledge of these subjects is useful, if we spend too much researching the subjects, we can become prisoners of the mind, which cuts us off from the spiritual and energetic realities.

Ascension: This is the process of reducing the dominance of the ego over our awareness and thoughts. This creates room for us to notice our increasing soul-infused spiritual presence as it grows and transforms our energies and consciousness. "Planetary Ascension" refers to the spiritual growth connected to human spiritual consciousness. "Galactic Ascension", or "Galactic Consciousness" refers to higher levels of ascension that go beyond typical human experiences and involve the higher self, spirit, light beings, and previously unknown levels of spiritual reality.

Polarity: This refers to the overriding experience of the physical universe, which is that everything has two poles or opposites such as night / day, life / death, or love / hate. The experience of polarity is not so present on the soul plane and can cause us problems when we incarnate in the psychical universe. This is because we tend to be attracted to one pole or the other, and this causes imbalances in different areas of life, as well as distorted views about spiritual reality which, in turn, does not experience polarity in the same way.

Soul: This is your spiritual essence, the aspect of you that gives yourself life. For me this part of us is a pure energy that experiences life in spiritual and emotional ways, but, interestingly, not in intellectual ways.

Higher Self: Whilst definitions of the Higher Self vary, for me the consciousness and experiences of each life are not lost after every life. They accumulate and create this immense, wise, and knowledgeable aspect of self that we call the Higher Self.

22 Freedom: Transcending Fate

Linked to the Tarot card the Wheel of Fortune number 10.

Whilst the Wheel of Fortune card (10) described a change in fortune, this higher card number 22, indicates a liberation from the wheel in which we begin to sense what it is like to be more able to create our own future through our thoughts and actions.

The energy of this higher Major Arcana energy gives us a great sense of peace as we no longer feel the tension caused by fate pulling and pushing us in different directions.

Suggested astrological link: The Constellation of Cygnus.

Suggested Colour: Ultraviolet.

23 GATEWAYS

23 Gateways: Worlds Within Worlds

Linked to the Tarot card Justice number 11.

The Justice card represents balance and harmony, which in terms of human spiritual consciousness, shows us the truth of who we are when the magnetic forces of a polarised physical universe are removed. The Gateways card takes this further by transcending polarity itself, revealing previously hidden dimensions of spiritual reality.

The energy of this higher Major Arcana energy gives us a great sense of new possibilities to connecting with other dimensions of consciousness, and even different spiritual realms. It evokes the emotion of excitement and a sense that mysterious worlds are waiting for us.

Suggested astrological link: The Star Bellatrix in the Orion constellation.

Suggested Colour: Purple.

24 SOUL

24 Soul Merge

Linked to the Tarot card the Hanged Man number 12.

The Hanged Man card (12) in terms of human spiritual consciousness, describes the willing descent of the soul to Earth to gain wisdom.

This higher card number 24, expands on this theme by describing how the soul willingly merges, in part, with the energy of Earth. This is a natural part of spiritual evolution, for spiritually advanced human souls. As this is the last card in this group, it represents a type of conclusion, which in this case, is a deep demonstration of appreciation and love before the soul moves on to the next level of Major Arcana energies represented by cards 25- 36. Past Masters who have experienced this include Mary Magdalene and we can still sense her spiritual presence linked to Earth, even though she has moved on from her lifetimes on Earth.

The energy of the soul merge card radiates the emotions of deep spiritual joy and love, reflecting this soulful connection to the planet and all its inhabitants.

Suggested astrological link: The Star Sirius B.

Suggested Colour: Magenta.

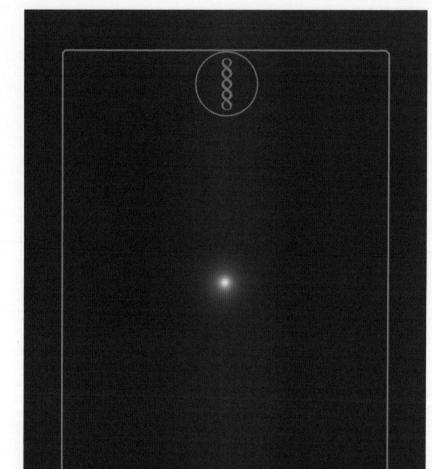

25 REGENERATION

25 Regeneration

Linked to the Tarot card Death number 13.

The Death card number 13, in terms of human spiritual consciousness, describes the end of the level of consciousness which Tarot cards 12-24 represent.

This higher Regeneration card number 25 expands on this theme by describing how at this higher level we are "reborn" into a life of higher consciousness that I would call Galactic consciousness. At this level we experience themes of growth that are less connected to Earth and, instead, we experience more, even deeper, spiritual realities.

The energy of the regeneration card gives us a sense of stillness and emptiness. We are purified and our higher consciousness, less distracted by earthly matters, can now explore a vast potential for new beginnings to be born from this place in our awareness.

Suggested astrological link: The Star Alcyone in the Pleiades Constellation.

Suggested Colour: Mid Blue.

26 EVOLVE

31

26 Evolve

Linked to the Tarot card the Temperance number 16.

The Temperance card (14), in terms of human spiritual consciousness, describes the spiritual process of Alchemy.

This higher card number 26 expands on this theme by describing how we embark on a new journey of expansion, and a time of experiencing new realities, which we merge with our current consciousness and energies, in dynamic ways.

The energy of the Evolve card gives us a powerful impulse to explore and engage with new spiritual realities in deeper ways than before. This is more than excitement; it is a compelling motivation to expand.

Suggested astrological link: The Star of Alnitak in the Orion Constellation.

Suggested Colour: Gold.

27 Spirit

Linked to the Tarot card the Devil card number 15.

The Devil card (15), in terms of human spiritual consciousness, describes willing devotion to a higher power.

This higher card number 27 expands on this theme by describing how we open up ourselves up to spirit and divine purpose.

The energy of the Spirit card gives us a powerful impulse to merge with spirit in dynamic and purposeful ways. This card is linked to spiritual service work.

Suggested astrological link: The Star of Rigel in the Orion Constellation.

Suggested Colour: Orange / Yellow.

28 Majesty

Linked to the Tarot card the Tower card number 16.

The Tower card (16), in terms of human spiritual consciousness, describes the receiving of spiritual illumination and enlightenment.

This higher card no 28, expands on this theme and those of the Emperor card number 4, by describing how we embrace and embody our newfound knowledge and wisdom. In this energy we are no longer just the receiver of wisdom and knowledge, but the source of it for others.

The energy of the Majesty card sets us on the course of the fulfilment of our potential. In this energy we no longer doubt, procrastinate or allow confusion to hold us back.

Suggested astrological link: The Star of Alnilam in the Constellation of Orion.

Suggested Colour: Royal Blue.

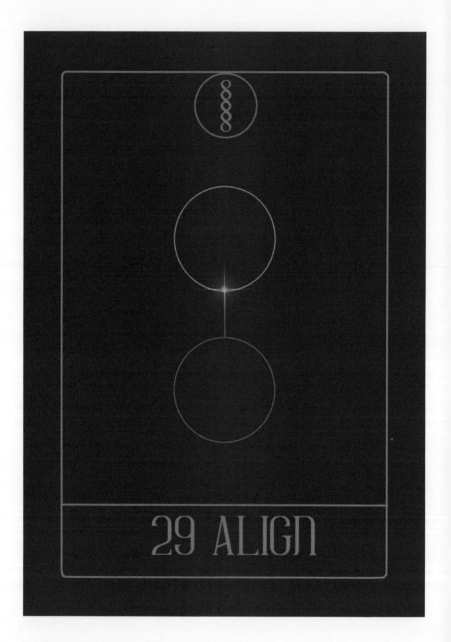

29 ALIGN

29 Align

Linked to the Tarot card the Star card number 17.

The Star card (17) in terms of human spiritual consciousness, describes how we connect to a higher spiritual guidance.

This higher card no 29 expands on this theme by describing how we surrender in spiritual terms and allow the spiritual guidance and blessings into our life without resistance.

The energy of the Align card puts us into a state of bliss, as we give up our battle with life and allow a natural state of grace to replace this.

Suggested astrological link: The Star of Betelgeuse in the Constellation of Orion.

Suggested Colour: White.

30 UNIVERSAL

39

30 Universal

Linked to the Tarot card the Moon card number 18.

The Moon card (18) in terms of human spiritual consciousness, describes the beginning of the spiritual process of ego dissolution (death of the ego).

This higher card Universal number 30 expands on this theme by describing how at this higher level, we identify much less with the self(ego) and our energies and consciousness are no longer centred on Earth. We become more universal in our identity, meaning we sense our spiritual realities as a soul, Higher Self and human being.

The energy of the Universal card is powerful and expansive. It gives us access to the deep spiritual experience of a higher reality where we are "everywhere" across all space and time.

Suggested astrological link: The Galaxy of Andromeda.

Suggested Colour: Multi coloured.

31 COMPASSION

31 Compassion

Linked to the Tarot card the Sun card number 19.

The Sun card (19), in terms of human spiritual consciousness, describes the emergence of a being awakening to its true glorious qualities and potentials.

This higher card number 31 expands on this theme by describing how we allow the expansion of our most scared aspect: the spiritual heart.

The energy of the Compassion card encapsulates the unconditional loving and caring nature of the spiritual heart in all its glory.

Suggested astrological link: The Star of Vega in the Lyra Constellation.

Suggested Colour: Pink / Orange.

32 HIGHER SELF

32 Higher Self

Linked to the Tarot card Judgement number 20.

The Judgement card (20), in terms of human spiritual consciousness, describes a spiritual awakening.

This higher card no 32 expands on this theme by describing how we complete the ongoing process of merging with our Higher Self.

The energy of Higher Self describes this ecstatic union and gives us the sense of ultimate wellbeing. We feel alive and perceive the realisation of our immortal spiritual reality.

Suggested astrological link: Unknown.

Suggested Colour: White.

EƎ MER KA BA

33 Mer Ka Ba

Linked to the Tarot card the World number 21.

The World card number 21, in terms of human spiritual consciousness, describes the emergence of a being awakening to its true glorious qualities and potentials.

This higher card no 33 expands on this theme by describing how we fully embrace our power over our energies and consciousness by working in unified ways with our Light Spirit Body (Mer Ka Ba).

The energy of Mer Ka Ba is a powerful, interactive energy, which we can use to work with energetic balance.

Suggested astrological link: Unknown.

Suggested Colour: Black.

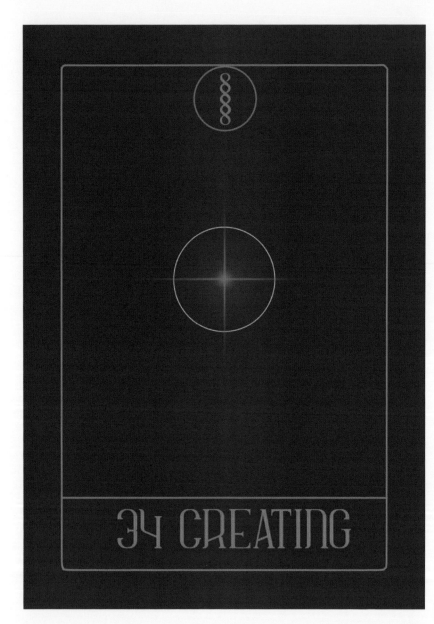

34 CREATING

34 Creating

Linked to my Lost Arcana card Freedom number 22.

The Freedom card number 22 in terms of human spiritual consciousness, describes a liberation from the Wheel of Fortune in which we begin to sense what it is like to be more able to create our own future through our thoughts and actions.

This higher Creating card no 34 expands on this theme by describing how in this energy, rather than being dominated by the ups and downs of fortune, we become more of a creator force, creating important and new potentials for ourselves and others.

The energy of the Creating card brings a sense of liberation from restriction, and a powerful ability to create new experiences in life.

Suggested astrological link: All Stars.

Suggested Colour: Gold.

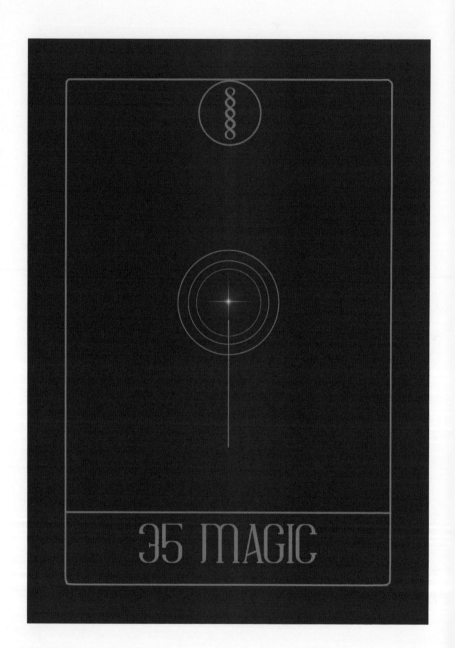

35 MAGIC

35 Magic

Linked to my Lost Arcana card Gateways number 23.

The Gateways card (19), in terms of human spiritual consciousness, transcends polarity itself, revealing previously hidden dimensions of spiritual reality.

This higher card Magic number 35 expands on this theme by introducing an energy that gives us an unlimited ability to travel in energy and consciousness. "As if by Magic", we sense the pull of the unknown and a newfound ability to explore new mysterious worlds. The epitome of this energy and card is Merlin.

The energy of the Magic card is very expansive and gives us a sense that all things are possible.

Suggested astrological link: The star of Alnilam in the Orion Constellation.

Suggested Colour: Dark Purple.

36 LIGHT BEING

36 Light Being

Linked to my Lost Arcana card Soul Merge number 24.

The Soul Merge card (24) in terms of human spiritual consciousness, describes how the soul willingly merges in part with the energy of Earth.

This higher card number 36 expands on this theme by describing how we merge into the light as a light being, whilst still being a physical human being.

The energy of the Light Being card gives us a sense of profound unlimited spiritual love, whilst experiencing the simultaneous realities as a human being and a light being. The epitome of this card can be found in the light beings of Asgard.

Suggested astrological link: Unknown.

Suggested Colour: Silver.

What next?

If you have enjoyed the contents of this book and want to learn more, then please visit my website to see information about my other Tarot books and my unique Tarot readings. These personal readings use the approaches I have described in this book to shed light on how Major Arcana energies influence your experiences of life and spiritual realities.

https://newarcanatarot.com/

AND PLEASE …

If you liked this book and want to see more of my writing in the future, I'd really appreciate a review on Amazon. The number of reviews a book receives has a direct impact on how it sells. Just leaving a review, no matter how short, helps make it possible for me to continue to do what I do.

Paul McCarthy

Printed in Great Britain
by Amazon

19897407R00033